REFUSING HEAVEN

REFUSING HEAVEN

POEMS BY

JACK GILBERT

ALFRED A. KNOPF   NEW YORK 2006

THIS IS A BORZOI BOOK
PUBLISHED BY ALFRED A. KNOPF

The following poems first appeared in *The New Yorker:* "Résumé," "Bring in the Gods,"
"Transgressions," "A Brief for the Defense," "By Small and Small: Midnight to Four A.M.," "What
to Want," and an earlier version of "A Kind of Courage" (as "Trying to Sleep").

Library of Congress Cataloging-in-Publication Data
Gilbert, Jack, [date]
Refusing heaven : poems / by Jack Gilbert.—1st ed.
p.   cm.
ISBN 1-4000-4365-4
I. Title.
PS3557.I34217R44 2005
813'.54—dc22   2004048844

Manufactured in the United States of America
Published March 11, 2005
Reprinted Two Times
Fourth Printing, January 2006

For Linda Gregg and Michiko Nogami

CONTENTS

REFUSING HEAVEN

A BRIEF FOR THE DEFENSE

Sorrow everywhere. Slaughter everywhere. If babies
are not starving someplace, they are starving
somewhere else. With flies in their nostrils.
But we enjoy our lives because that's what God wants.
Otherwise the mornings before summer dawn would not
be made so fine. The Bengal tiger would not
be fashioned so miraculously well. The poor women
at the fountain are laughing together between
the suffering they have known and the awfulness
in their future, smiling and laughing while somebody
in the village is very sick. There is laughter
every day in the terrible streets of Calcutta,
and the women laugh in the cages of Bombay.
If we deny our happiness, resist our satisfaction,
we lessen the importance of their deprivation.
We must risk delight. We can do without pleasure,
but not delight. Not enjoyment. We must have
the stubbornness to accept our gladness in the ruthless
furnace of this world. To make injustice the only
measure of our attention is to praise the Devil.
If the locomotive of the Lord runs us down,
we should give thanks that the end had magnitude.
We must admit there will be music despite everything.
We stand at the prow again of a small ship
anchored late at night in the tiny port
looking over to the sleeping island: the waterfront
is three shuttered cafés and one naked light burning.
To hear the faint sound of oars in the silence as a rowboat
comes slowly out and then goes back is truly worth
all the years of sorrow that are to come.

NAKED EXCEPT FOR THE JEWELRY

"And," she said, "you must talk no more
about ecstasy. It is a loneliness."
The woman wandered about picking up
her shoes and silks. "You said you loved me,"
the man said. "We tell lies," she said,
brushing her wonderful hair, naked except
for the jewelry. "We try to believe."
"You were helpless with joy," he said,
"moaning and weeping." "In the dream," she said,
"we pretend to ourselves that we are touching.
The heart lies to itself because it must."

PUT HER IN THE FIELDS FOR KINDNESS

The door was in the whitewashed eight-foot walls
of the narrow back street common to Greek islands.
Beautiful light and shade in the clear air.
The big iron bolt was on the outside locking
something in. Some days the pounding inside
made the heavy wooden door shudder. Often a voice
screaming. The crazy old woman, people said.
She would hurt the children if they let her out.
Pinch them or scare them, they said.
Sometimes everything was still and I would delay
until I heard the tiny whimper that meant she knew
I was there. Late one afternoon on my way for oil,
the door was broken. She was in the lot opposite
in weeds by the wall, her dress pulled up, pissing.
Like a cow. Able to manage, quiet in the last light.

WHAT SONG SHOULD WE SING

The massive overhead crane comes
when we wave to it, lets down
its heavy claws and waits tamely
within its power while we hook up
the slabs of three-quarter-inch
steel. Takes away the ponderous
reality when we wave again.
What name do we have for that?
What song is there for its voice?
What is the other face of Yahweh?
The god who made the slug and ferret,
the maggot and shark in his image.
What is the carol for that?
Is it the song of nevertheless,
or of the empire of our heart? We carry
language as our mind, but are we
the dead whale that sinks grandly
for years to reach the bottom of us?

HAVING THE HAVING

I tie knots in the strings of my spirit
to remember. They are not pictures
of what was. Not accounts of dusk
amid the olive trees and that odor.
The walking back was the arriving.
For that there are three knots
and a space and another two
close together. They do not imitate
the inside of her body, nor her clean
mouth. They cannot describe, but they
can prevent remembering it wrong.
The knots recall. The knots
are blazons marking the trail
back to what we own and imperfectly
forget. Back to a bell ringing
far off, and the sweet summer darkening.
All but a little of it blurs and leaks
away, but that little is most of it,
even damaged. Two more knots
and then just straight string.

SAY YOU LOVE ME

Are the angels of her bed the angels
who come near me alone in mine?
Are the green trees in her window
the color I see in ripe plums?
If she always sees backward
and upside down without knowing it
what chance do we have? I am haunted
by the feeling that she is saying
melting lords of death, avalanches,
rivers and moments of passing through.
And I am replying, "Yes, yes.
Shoes and pudding."

KUNSTKAMMER

We are resident inside with the machinery,
a glimmering spread throughout the apparatus.
We exist with a wind whispering inside
and our moon flexing. Amid the ducts,
inside the basilica of bones. The flesh
is a neighborhood, but not the life.
Our body is not good at memory, at keeping.
It is the spirit that holds on to our treasure.
The dusk in Italy when the ferry passed Bellagio
and turned across Lake Como in the hush to where
we would land and start up the grassy mountain.
The body keeps so little of the life after
being with her eleven years,
and the mouth not even that much. But the heart
is different. It never forgets
the pine trees with the moon rising behind them
every night. Again and again we put our
sweet ghosts on small paper boats and sailed
them back into their death, each moving slowly
into the dark, disappearing as our hearts
visited and savored, hurt and yearned.

HALLOWEEN

There were a hundred wild people in Allen's
three-story house. He was sitting at a small
table in the kitchen quietly eating something.
Alone, except for Orlovsky's little brother
who was asleep with his face against the wall.
Allen wearing a red skullcap, and a loose bathrobe
over his nakedness. Shoulder-length hair
and a chest-length, oily beard.
No one was within fifteen years of him. Destroyed
like the rest of that clan. His remarkable
talent destroyed. The fine mind grown more
and more simple. Buddhist chants, impoverishing
poems. There are no middle tones in the paintings
of children. Chekhov said he didn't want
the audience to cry, but to see. Allen showing
me his old man's bald scalp. A kind of love.
Aachen is a good copy of a mediocre building.
Architects tried for two thousand years to find
a way to put a dome on a square base.

ELEGY FOR BOB (JEAN McLEAN)

Only you and I still stand in the snow on Highland Avenue
in Pittsburgh waiting for the blundering iron streetcars
that never came. Only you know how the immense storms
over the Allegheny and Monongahela rivers were the scale
I wanted. Nobody but you remembers Peabody High School.
You shared my youth in Paris and the hills above Como.
And later, in Seattle. It was you playing the aria from
Don Giovanni over and over, filling the forest of Puget
Sound with the music. You in the front room and me
upstairs with your discarded wife in my bed. The sound
of your loneliness pouring over our happy bodies.
You were with your third wife when I was in Perugia
six months later, but were in love with somebody else.
We searched for her in Munich, the snow falling again.
You trying to decide when to kill yourself. All of it
finally bringing us to San Francisco. To the vast
decaying white house. No sound of Mozart coming up
from there. No alleluias in you anymore. No longer
will you waltz under the chandeliers in Paris salons
drunk with champagne and the Greek girl as the others
stand along the mirrored walls. The men watching
with fury, the eyes of the women inscrutable. No one
else speaks the language of those years. No one
remembers you as the Baron. The streetcars have
finished the last run, and I am walking home. Thinking
love is not refuted because it comes to an end.

RÉSUMÉ

Easter on the mountain. The hanging goat roasted
with lemon, pepper and thyme. The American hacks off
the last of the meat, gets out the remaining
handfuls from the spine. Grease up to the elbows,
his face smeared and his heart blooming. The satisfied
farmers watch his fervor with surprise.
When the day begins to cool, he makes his way down
the trails. Down from that holiday energy
to the silence of his real life, where he will
wash in cold water by kerosene light, happy
and alone. A future inch by inch, rock by rock,
by the green wheat and the ripe wheat later.
By basil and dove tower and white doves turning
in the brilliant sky. The ghosts of his other world
crowding around, surrounding him with himself.
Tomato by tomato, canned fish in the daily stew.
He sits outside on the wall of his vineyard
as night rises from the parched earth and the sea
darkens in the distance. Insistent stars and him
singing in the quiet. Flesh of the spirit and soul
of the body. The clarity that does so much damage.

MORE THAN SIXTY

Out of money, so I'm sitting in the shade
of my farmhouse cleaning the lentils
I found in the back of the cupboard.
Listening to the cicada in the fig tree
mix with the cooing doves on the roof.
I look up when I hear a goat hurt far down
the valley and discover the sea
exactly the same blue I used to paint it
with my watercolors as a child.
So what, I think happily. So what!

BY SMALL AND SMALL:
MIDNIGHT TO FOUR A.M.

For eleven years I have regretted it,
regretted that I did not do what
I wanted to do as I sat there those
four hours watching her die. I wanted
to crawl in among the machinery
and hold her in my arms, knowing
the elementary, leftover bit of her
mind would dimly recognize it was me
carrying her to where she was going.

ONCE UPON A TIME

We were young incidentally, stumbling
into joy, he said. The sweetness of
our bodies was natural in the way
the sun came out of the Mediterranean
fresh every morning. We were accidentally
alive. A shape without a form.
We were a music composed of melody,
without chords, played only on
the white keys. We thought excitement
was love, that intensity was a marriage.
We meant no harm, but could see the women
only a little through the ardor and hurry.
We were innocent, he said, baffled when
they let us kiss their tender mouths.
Sometimes they kissed back, even volunteered.

A CLOSE CALL

Dusk and the sea is thus and so. The cat
from two fields away crossing through the grapes.
It is so quiet I can hear the air
in the canebrake. The blond wheat darkens.
The glaze is gone from the bay and the heat lets go.
They have not lit the lamp at the other farm yet
and all at once I feel lonely. What a surprise.
But the air stills, the heat comes back
and I think I am all right again.

THE ROOSTER

They have killed the rooster, thank God,
but it's strange to have my half
of the valley unreported. Without the rooster
it's like my place by the Chinese elm is not here
each day. As though I'm gone. I touch my face
and get up to make tea, feeling my heart claim
no territory. Like the colorless weeds which fail,
but don't give in. Silent in the world's clamor.
They killed the rooster because he could feel
nothing for the six frumpy hens. Now there is only
the youngster to announce and cover. They are only
aunts to him. Mostly he works on his crowing. And for
a long time the roosters on the other farms would not
answer. But yesterday they started laying
full-throated performances on him. He would come
back, but couldn't get the hang of it. The scorn
and the failing went on until finally one day,
from the other end of the valley, came a deep
voice saying, "For Christ's sake, kid, like this."
And it began. Not bothering to declare parts
of the landscape, but announcing the glory,
the greatness of the sun and moon.
Told of the heavenly hosts, the mysteries,
and the joy. Which were the Huns and which not.
Describing the dominions of wind and song. What was
noble in all things. It was very quiet after that.

FAILING AND FLYING

Everyone forgets that Icarus also flew.
It's the same when love comes to an end,
or the marriage fails and people say
they knew it was a mistake, that everybody
said it would never work. That she was
old enough to know better. But anything
worth doing is worth doing badly.
Like being there by that summer ocean
on the other side of the island while
love was fading out of her, the stars
burning so extravagantly those nights that
anyone could tell you they would never last.
Every morning she was asleep in my bed
like a visitation, the gentleness in her
like antelope standing in the dawn mist.
Each afternoon I watched her coming back
through the hot stony field after swimming,
the sea light behind her and the huge sky
on the other side of that. Listened to her
while we ate lunch. How can they say
the marriage failed? Like the people who
came back from Provence (when it was Provence)
and said it was pretty but the food was greasy.
I believe Icarus was not failing as he fell,
but just coming to the end of his triumph.

BURNING (ANDANTE NON TROPPO)

We are all burning in time, but each is consumed
at his own speed. Each is the product
of his spirit's refraction, of the inflection
of that mind. It is the pace of our living
that makes the world available. Regardless of
the body's lion-wrath or forest waiting, despite
the mind's splendid appetite or the sad power
in our soul's separation from God and women,
it is always our gait of being that decides
how much is seen, what the mystery of us knows,
and what the heart will smell of the landscape
as the Mexican train continues at a dog-trot each
day going north. The grand Italian churches are
covered with detail which is visible at the pace
people walk by. The great modern buildings are
blank because there is no time to see from the car.
A thousand years ago when they built the gardens
of Kyoto, the stones were set in the streams askew.
Whoever went quickly would fall in. When we slow,
the garden can choose what we notice. Can change
our heart. On the wall of a toilet in Rock Springs
years ago there was a dispenser that sold tubes of
cream to numb a man's genitals. Called Linger.

THE OTHER PERFECTION

Nothing here. Rock and fried earth.
Everything destroyed by the fierce light.
Only stones and small fields of
stubborn barley and lentils. No broken
things to repair. Nothing thrown away
or abandoned. If you want a table,
you pay a man to make it. If you find two
feet of barbed wire, you take it home.
You'll need it. The farmers don't laugh.
They go to town to laugh, or to fiestas.
A kind of paradise. Everything itself.
The sea is water. Stones are made of rock.
The sun goes up and goes down. A success
without any enhancement whatsoever.

A BALL OF SOMETHING

Watching the ant walk under water along
the bottom of my saucepan is painful.
Though he seems in no distress.
He walks at leisure, almost strolling.
Lifts his head twice in the solid outside
and goes on. Until he encounters a bit
of something and acts almost afraid
in struggling to get free. After, he continues,
again at ease. He looks up and pitches forward
into a tight ball. It is not clear whether
that's the end. Perhaps he is doing what
the hedgehog does well. Waiting for someone
to go by whose ankle he can grab
and ask for help. Hoping for pity. But maybe
not. Maybe he lies there curled around a smile,
liberated at last. Dreaming of coming back
as Byron, or maybe the favorite dog.

GETTING AWAY WITH IT

We have already lived in the real paradise.
Horses in the empty summer street.
Me eating the hot wurst I couldn't afford,
in frozen Munich, tears dropping. We can
remember. A child in the outfield waiting
for the last fly ball of the year. So dark
already it was black against heaven.
The voices trailing away to dinner,
calling faintly in the immense distance.
Standing with my hands open, watching it
curve over and start down, turning white
at the last second. Hands down. Flourishing.

TRUTH

The glare of the Greek sun
on our stone house
is not so white
as the pale moonlight on it.

TRANSGRESSIONS

He thinks about how important the sinning was,
how much his equity was in simply being alive.
Like the sloth. The days and nights wasted,
doing nothing important adding up to
the favorite years. Long hot afternoons
watching ants while the cicadas railed
in the Chinese elm about the brevity of life.
Indolence so often when no one was watching.
Wasting June mornings with the earth singing
all around. Autumn afternoons doing nothing
but listening to the siren voices of streams
and clouds coaxing him into the sweet happiness
of leaving all of it alone. Using up what
little time we have, relishing our mortality,
waltzing slowly without purpose. Neglecting
the future. Content to let the garden fail
and the house continue on in its usual disorder.
Yes, and coveting his neighbors' wives.
Their clean hair and soft voices. The seraphim
he was sure were in one of the upstairs rooms.
Hesitant occasions of pride, feeling himself feeling.
Waking in the night and lying there. Discovering
the past in the wonderful stillness. The other,
older pride. Watching the ambulance take away
the man whose throat he had crushed. Above all,
his greed. Greed of time, of being. This world,
the pine woods stretching all brown or bare
on either side of the railroad tracks in the winter
twilight. Him feeling the cold, sinfully unshriven.

THE ABANDONED VALLEY

Can you understand being alone so long
you would go out in the middle of the night
and put a bucket into the well
so you could feel something down there
tug at the other end of the rope?

HAPPENING APART FROM WHAT'S HAPPENING AROUND IT

There is a vividness to eleven years of love
because it is over. A clarity of Greece now
because I live in Manhattan or New England.
If what is happening is part of what's going on
around what's occurring, it is impossible
to know what is truly happening. If love is
part of the passion, part of the fine food
or the villa on the Mediterranean, it is not
clear what the love is. When I was walking
in the mountains with the Japanese man and began
to hear the water, he said, "What is the sound
of the waterfall?" "Silence," he finally told me.
The stillness I did not notice until the sound
of water falling made apparent the silence I had
been hearing long before. I ask myself what
is the sound of women? What is the word for
that still thing I have hunted inside them
for so long? Deep inside the avalanche of joy,
the thing deeper in the dark, and deeper still
in the bed where we are lost. Deeper, deeper
down where a woman's heart is holding its breath,
where something very far away in that body
is becoming something we don't have a name for.

EXCEEDING THE SPIRIT

Beyond what the fires have left of the cathedral
you can see old men standing here and there
in administration buildings looking out
of the fine casements with the glass gone.
Idle and bewildered. The few people who are
in the weed-choked streets below carry things
without purpose, holding fading memories inside
of what the good used to be. Immense ships
rise in the distance, beached and dying.
Starving men crouch in the dirt of the plaza with
a scrap of cloth before them, trying to sell nothing:
one with dead fuses and a burnt-out lightbulb,
another with just a heavy bolt and screw
rusted together. One has two Byzantine coins
and a lump of oxidation which has a silver piece
inside stamped with the face of Hermes, but he
doesn't know it. A strange place to look for
what matters, what is worthy. To arrive now
at the wilderness alone and striving harder
for discontent, to need again. Not for salvation.
To go on because there might be something like him.
To visit what is importantly unknown of what is.

MEDITATION ELEVEN:
READING BLAKE AGAIN

I remember that house I'd rented with them.
The laughing and constant talk of love.
The energy of their friends.
And the sounds late at night.
The sound of whipping. Urging and screams.
Like the dead lying to each other.

HOW MUCH OF THAT IS LEFT IN ME?

Yearning inside the rejoicing. The heart's famine
within the spirit's joy. Waking up happy
and practicing discontent. Seeing the poverty
in the perfection, but still hungering
for its strictness. Thinking of
a Greek farmer in the orchard,
the white almond blossoms falling and falling
on him as he struggled with his wooden plow.
I remember the stark and precious winters in Paris.
Just after the war when everyone was poor and cold.
I walked hungry through the vacant streets at night
with the snow falling wordlessly in the dark like petals
on the last of the nineteenth century. Substantiality
seemed so near in the grand empty boulevards,
while the famous bronze bells told of time.
Stripping everything down until being was visible.
The ancient buildings and the Seine,
small stone bridges and regal fountains flourishing
in the emptiness. What fine provender in the want.
What freshness in me amid the loneliness.

'TIS HERE! 'TIS HERE! 'TIS GONE!
(THE NATURE OF PRESENCE)

A white horse, Linda Gregg wrote, is not a horse,
quoting what Hui Shih said twenty-three hundred
years ago. The thing is not its name, is not
the words. The painting of a pipe is not a pipe
regardless of what the title claims. An intelligent
poet in Iowa is frightened because she thinks
we are made of electrons. The Gianna Gelmetti
I loved was a presence ignited in a swarm
of energy, but the ghost living in the mansion
is not the building. Consciousness is not
matter dreaming. If all the stars were added
together they would still not know it's spring.
The silence of the mountain is not our silence.
The sound of the earth will never be *Un Bel Di*.
We are a contingent occurrence. The white horse
in moonlight is more white than when it stands
in sunlight. And even then it depends on whether
a bell is ringing. The intimate body of the Valerie
I know is not the secret body my friend knows.
The luster of her breasts is conditional:
clothed or not, desired or too familiar.
The fact of them is mediated by morning
or the depth of night when it's pouring down rain.
The reason we cannot enter the same woman
twice is not because the mesh of energy flexes.

It is a mystery separate from both matter
and electrons. It is not why the Linda
looking out over the Aegean is not the Linda
eating melon in Kentucky, nor explains how
the mind lives amid the rain without being
part of it. The dead lady Nogami-san lives now
only in me, in the momentary occasion I am.
Her whiteness in me is the color of pale amber
in winter light.

AMBITION

Having reached the beginning, starting toward
a new ignorance. Places to become,
secrets to live in, sins to achieve.
Maybe South America, perhaps a new woman,
another language to not understand.
Like setting out on a raft over an ocean
of life already well lived.
A two-story failed hotel in the tropics,
hot silence of noon with the sun
straying through the shutters.
Sitting with his poems at a small table,
everybody asleep. Thinking with pleasure,
trailing his hand in the river he will
turn into.

BEING YOUNG BACK THEN

Another beautiful love letter
trying to win her back. Finished,
like each night, just before dawn.
Down the Corso Garibaldi to the Piazza
Fortebraccio. Across to the massive
Etruscan gate and up the Via
Ulisse Rocchi. To the main square.
Past the cathedral, past the fountain
of Nicola Pisano. And the fine
eleventh-century town hall.
To the post office so the letter
could get to California in three days.
Then to the palazzo to stand always
for a half hour looking up to where
Gianna was sleeping. Longing for
her and dreaming of the other one.

NOT GETTING CLOSER

Walking in the dark streets of Seoul
under the almost full moon.
Lost for the last two hours.
Finishing a loaf of bread
and worried about the curfew.
I have not spoken for three days
and I am thinking, "Why not just
settle for love? Why not just
settle for love instead?"

ADULTS

The sea lies in its bed wet and naked
in the dark. Half a moon glimmers on it
as though someone had come through
a door with the light behind. The woman thinks
of how they lived in the neighborhood
for years while she belonged to other men.
He moves toward her knowing he is about to
spoil the way they didn't know each other.

SEEN FROM ABOVE

In the end, Hannibal walked out of his city
saying the Romans wanted only him. Why should
his soldiers make love to their swords?
He walked out alone, a small figure in
the great field, his elephants dead at
the bottom of the Alps' crevasses. So might we
go to our Roman death in triumph. Our love
is of marble and large tawny roses,
in the endless harvests of our defeat.
We have slept with death all our lives.
It will grind out its graceless victory,
but we can limp in triumph over the cold
intervening sand.

GETTING CLOSER

The heat's on the bus with us.
The icon in front, the chunk
of raw meat in the rack
on the other side. The boy
languid in the seat under it
rubbing his eyes. Old women
talking almost softly.
Quietly, I look in the bus waiting
next to us and meet the eyes
of a pretty Greek girl.
She looks back steadily.
I drop my eyes and the bus
drives away.

THE MAIL

What the hell are you doing out there
(he writes) in that worn rock valley
with chickens and the donkey and not farming?
And the people around you speaking Greek.
And the only news faint on the Armed
Forces Network. I don't know what to say.
And what about women? he asks. Yes,
I think to myself, what about women?

LESS BEING MORE

It started when he was a young man
and went to Italy. He climbed mountains,
wanting to be a poet. But was troubled
by what Dorothy Wordsworth wrote in
her journal about William having worn
himself out searching all day to find
a simile for nightingale. It seemed
a long way from the tug of passion.
He ended up staying in pensioni
where the old women would take up
the children in the middle of the night
to rent the room, carrying them warm
and clinging to the mothers, the babies
making a mewing sound. He began hunting
for the second rate. The insignificant
ruins, the negligible museums, the back-
country villages with only one pizzeria
and two small bars. The unimproved.

HOMAGE TO WANG WEI

An unfamiliar woman sleeps on the other side
of the bed. Her faint breathing is like a secret
alive inside her. They had known each other
three days in California four years ago. She was
engaged and got married afterwards. Now the winter
is taking down the last of the Massachusetts leaves.
The two o'clock Boston and Maine goes by,
calling out of the night like trombones rejoicing,
leaving him in the silence after. She cried yesterday
when they walked in the woods, but she didn't want
to talk about it. Her suffering will be explained,
but she will be unknown nevertheless. Whatever happens,
he will not find her. Despite the tumult and trespass
they might achieve in the wilderness of their bodies
and the voices of the heart clamoring, they will still
be a mystery each to the other, and to themselves.

THE BUTTERNUT TREE AT FORT JUNIPER

I called the tree a butternut (which I don't think
it is) so I could talk about how different
the trees are around me here in the rain.
It reminds me how mutable language is. Keats
would leave blank places in his drafts to hold on
to his passion, spaces for the right words to come.
We use them sideways. The way we automatically
add bits of shape to hold on to the dissolving dreams.
So many of the words are for meanwhile. We say,
"I love you" while we search for language
that can be heard. Which allows us to talk
about how the aspens over there tremble
in the smallest shower, while the tree over by
the window here gathers the raindrops and lets them
go in bunches. The way my heart carols sometimes,
and other times yearns. Sometimes is quiet
and other times is powerfully quiet.

DOING POETRY

Poem, you sonofabitch, it's bad enough
that I embarrass myself working so hard
to get it right even a little,
and that little grudging and awkward.
But it's afterwards I resent, when
the sweet sure should hold me like
a trout in the bright summer stream.
There should be at least briefly
access to your glamour and tenderness.
But there's always this same old
dissatisfaction instead.

HOMESTEADING

It would be easy if the spirit
was reasonable, was old.
But there is a stubborn gladness.
Summer air idling in the elms.
Silence hunting in the towering
storms of heaven. Thirty-two
swans in a København dusk.
The swan bleeding to death
slowly in a Greek kitchen.
A man leaves the makeshift
restaurant plotting his improvidence.
Something voiceless flies lovely
over an empty landscape.
He wanders on the way
to whoever he will become.
Passion leaves us single and safe.
The other fervor leaves us
at risk, in love, and alone.
Married sometimes forever.

THE SWEET TASTE OF THE NIGHT

When I woke up my head was saying, "The world
will pardon my mush, but I've got a crush"
and I went outside. The wind was gone.
The last of the moon was just up and the stars
brighter even than usual. A freighter
in the distance was turning into the bay,
all lit up. The valley was so still I could
hear the engine. The dogs quiet, worn out barking
all week at the full moon. Their ease in failure.
The ship came out the other side of the hill
and blew its horn softly for the harbor.
Waking a rooster on the mountain. It went
behind the second hill and I started back inside
the farmhouse. "All the day and night time,
hear me cry. The world will pardon my emotion,"
I sang from my bed, up into the dark, my voice
unfamiliar after not speaking for days.
Thinking of Linda, but singing to something else.

HONOR

All honor at a distance is punctilio.
One dies dutifully by a code
which applies to nothing recognizable.
It is like the perfect grace of our
contessa who has been mad and foul
for the last thirty years.

TRYING TO WRITE POETRY

There is a wren sitting in the branches
of my spirit and it chooses not to sing.
It is listening to learn its song.
Sits in the Palladian light trying to decide
what it will sing when it is time to sing.
Tra la, tra la the other birds sing
in the morning, and silently when the snow
is slowly falling just before evening.
Knowing that passion is not a color
not confused by energy. The bird will sing
about summer having its affair with Italy.
Is frightened of classical singing.
Will sing happily of the color fruits are
in the cool dark, the wetness inside
overripe peaches, the smell of melons
and the briars that come with berries.
When the sun falls into silence,
the two birds will sing. Back and forth,
making a whole. Silence answering silence.
Song answering song. Gone and gone.
Gone somewhere. Gone nowhere.

A KIND OF COURAGE

The girl shepherd on the farm beyond has been
taken from school now she is twelve, and her life is over.
I got my genius brother a summer job in the mills
and he stayed all his life. I lived with a woman four
years who went crazy later, escaped from the hospital,
hitchhiked across America terrified and in the snow
without a coat. Was raped by most men who gave her
a ride. I crank my heart even so and it turns over.
Ranges high in the sun over continents and eruptions
of mortality, through winds and immensities of rain
falling for miles. Until all the world is overcome
by what goes up and up in us, singing and dancing
and throwing down flowers nevertheless.

HAPPILY PLANTING THE BEANS TOO EARLY

I waited until the sun was going down
to plant the bean seedlings. I was
beginning on the peas when the phone rang.
It was a long conversation about what
living this way in the woods might
be doing to me. It was dark by the time
I finished. Made tuna fish sandwiches
and read the second half of a novel.
Found myself out in the April moonlight
putting the rest of the pea shoots into
the soft earth. It was after midnight.
There was a bird calling intermittently
and I could hear the stream down below.
She was probably right about me getting
strange. After all, Bashō and Tolstoy
at the end were at least going somewhere.

WHAT TO WANT

The room was like getting married.
A landfall and the setting forth.
A dearness and vessel. A small room
eight by twelve, filled by the narrow iron bed.
Six stories up, under the roof
and no elevator. A maid's room long ago.
In the old quarter, on the other hill
with the famous city stretched out
below. His window like an ocean.
The great bells of the cathedral counting
the hours all night while everyone slept.
After two years, he had come to
the beginning. Past the villa at Como,
past the police moving him from jail
to jail to hide him from the embassy.
His first woman gone back to Manhattan,
the friends gone back to weddings
or graduate school. He was finally alone.
Without money. A wind blowing through
where much of him used to be. No longer
the habit of himself. The blinding intensity
giving way to presence. The budding
amid the random passion. Mortality like
a cello inside him. Like rain in the dark.
Sin a promise. What interested him
most was who he was about to become.

BRING IN THE GODS

Bring in the gods I say, and he goes out. When he comes
back and I know they are with him, I say, Put tables in front
of them so they be may be seated, and food upon the tables
so they may eat. When they have eaten, I ask which of them
will question me. Let him hold up his hand, I say.
The one on the left raises his hand and I tell him to ask.
Where are you now, he says. I stand on top of myself, I hear
myself answer. I stand on myself like a hilltop and my life
is spread before me. Does it surprise you, he asks. I explain
that in our youth and for a long time after our youth we cannot
see our lives. Because we are inside of that. Because we can
see no shape to it since we have nothing to compare it to.
We have not seen it grow and change because we are too close.
We don't know the names of things that would bind them to us,
so we cannot feed on them. One near the middle asks why not.
Because we don't have the knack for eating what we are living.
Why is that? she asks. Because we are too much in a hurry.
Where are you now? the one on the left says. With the ghosts.
I am with Gianna those two years in Perugia. Meeting secretly
in the thirteenth-century alleys of stone. Walking in the fields
through the spring light, she well dressed and walking in heels
over the plowed land. We are just outside the city walls
hidden under the thorny blackberry bushes and her breasts naked.
I am with her those many twilights in the olive orchards,
holding the heart of her as she whimpers. Now where are you?

he says. I am with Linda those years and years. In American
cities, in København, on Greek islands season after season.
Lindos and Monolithos and the other places. I am with Michiko
for eleven years, East and West, holding her clear in my mind
the way a native can hold all of his village at one moment.
Where are you now? he says. I am standing on myself the way
a bird sits in her nest, with the babies half asleep underneath
and the world all leaves and morning air. What do you want?
a blonde one asks. To keep what I already have, I say. You ask
too much, he says sternly. Then you are at peace, she says.
I am not at peace, I tell her. I want to fail. I am hungry
for what I am becoming. What will you do? she asks. I will
continue north, carrying the past in my arms, flying into winter.

THE NEGLIGIBLE

I lie in bed listening to it sing
in the dark about the sweetness
of brief love and the perfection of loves
that might have been. The spirit cherishes
the disregarded. It is because the body continues
to fail at remembering the smell of Michiko
that her body is so clear in me after all this time.
There is a special pleasure in remembering the shine
on her spoon merging with faint sounds
in the distance of her rising from the bathwater.

THE LOST HOTELS OF PARIS

The Lord gives everything and charges
by taking it back. What a bargain.
Like being young for a while. We are
allowed to visit hearts of women,
to go into their bodies so we feel
no longer alone. We are permitted
romantic love with its bounty and half-life
of two years. It is right to mourn
for the small hotels of Paris that used to be
when we used to be. My mansard looking
down on Notre Dame every morning is gone,
and me listening to the bell at night.
Venice is no more. The best Greek islands
have drowned in acceleration. But it's the having
not the keeping that is the treasure.
Ginsberg came to my house one afternoon
and said he was giving up poetry
because it told lies, that language distorts.
I agreed, but asked what we have
that gets it right even that much.
We look up at the stars and they are
not there. We see the memory
of when they were, once upon a time.
And that too is more than enough.

Him, she said, and him. They put us in the second car
and followed her back to the villa. Our fear slowly
faded during the weeks. Everyone was kind but busy.
We could go anywhere on the first floor
and on the grounds this side of the fence.
They decided on me and sent the other boy away.
Before I had only glimpsed her at the upper windows.
Now we ate together at opposite ends of the table.
Candlelight eased her age, but not her guilt.
Once she said the world was an astonishing animal:
light was its spirit and noise was its mind.
That it was composed to feed on honor, but did not.
Another time she warned me about walking on the lawns
at night. Told me of heavy birds that flew after dark
croaking, "Feathers or lead, stone or fire?"
Mounting people who gave the wrong answer and riding
them like horses across the whole county, beating them
with their powerful wings. We would play cards
silently on rainy days, and have sardine sandwiches
at four in the morning, taking turns reading aloud
from Tolstoy. "What need do we have for consulates?"
she said once before going upstairs, the grand room
beginning to fill with the dawn. "Why insist
on nature? A flower must be red or white, but we
can be anything. Our victories are difficult

because the triumph is not in possessing excellence.
It is found in reluctance." Month after month
we lived like that. And with me telling her
what it was like out there among the living.
She was steadily failing, like a Palladian palace
coming apart gracefully. The last morning she stood
by the tall windows. "I will not give you my blessing,"
she said, "and I refuse you also my reasons. Who are you,
who is anyone to make me just?" When they came for her,
she smiled at me and said, "At last."

WHAT PLENTY

Hitting each other. Backing up
and hitting each other again
in the loud silence of the stars
and the roar of their headlights.
Trying to force feeling and squeezing
out pain. Eden built of iron and grit.
Arcades fashioned entirely of guilt.
Paradise of loss, of lipsticked nipples,
lying to children about the soul.
Dead women stuffed with flowers.
Abandoned cabs in empty streets
not listening to the red lights,
yellow nor green.

THE GARDEN

We come from a deep forest of years
into a valley of an unknown country
called loneliness. Without horse or dog
the heavens bottomless overhead.
We are like Marco Polo who came back
with jewels hidden in the seams of his ragged clothes.
A sweet sadness, a tough happiness.
This beginner cobbles together a kind of house
and makes lentil soup there night
after night. Sits on the great stone
that is a threshold, smelling pine trees
in the hot darkness. When the moon rises
between the tall trunks, he sings without
talent but with pleasure. Then goes inside
to make courtesy with his dear ghosts.
In the morning, he watches the two nuthatches,
the pair of finches with their new son.
And the chickadees. There are chipmunks
in the afternoon finding seeds between
his fingers with their exquisite hands.
He visits his misbegotten garden where
the mint and chives flourish alongside
the few stunted tomatoes and eggplants.
They are scarce because of ignorance.
He wonders all the time where
he has arrived, why so much has been
allowed him (even rain on the leaves
of sugar maples), and why there is
even now so much to come.

MUSIC IS IN THE PIANO
ONLY WHEN IT IS PLAYED

We are not one with this world. We are not
the complexity our body is, nor the summer air
idling in the big maple without purpose.
We are a shape the wind makes in these leaves
as it passes through. We are not the wood
any more than the fire, but the heat which is a marriage
between the two. We are certainly not the lake
nor the fish in it, but the something that is
pleased by them. We are the stillness when
a mighty Mediterranean noon subtracts even the voices
of insects by the broken farmhouse. We are evident
when the orchestra plays, and yet are not part
of the strings or brass. Like the song that exists
only in the singing, and is not the singer.
God does not live among the church bells,
but is briefly resident there. We are occasional
like that. A lifetime of easy happiness mixed
with pain and loss, trying always to name and hold
on to the enterprise under way in our chest.
Reality is not what we marry as a feeling. It is what
walks up the dirt path, through the excessive heat
and giant sky, the sea stretching away.
He continues past the nunnery to the old villa
where he will sit on the terrace with her, their sides
touching. In the quiet that is the music of that place,
which is the difference between silence and windlessness.

WINNING ON THE BLACK

The silence is so complete he can hear
the whispers inside him. Mostly names
of women. Women gone or dead. The ones
we loved so easily. What is it, he wonders,
that we had then and don't have now,
that we once were and are no longer.
It seemed natural to be alive back then.
Soon there will be only the raccoon's
tracks in the snow down by the river.

REFUSING HEAVEN

The old women in black at early Mass in winter
are a problem for him. He could tell by their eyes
they have seen Christ. They make the kernel
of his being and the clarity around it
seem meager, as though he needs girders
to hold up his unusable soul. But he chooses
against the Lord. He will not abandon his life.
Not his childhood, not the ninety-two bridges
across the two rivers of his youth. Nor the mills
along the banks where he became a young man
as he worked. The mills are eaten away, and eaten
again by the sun and its rusting. He needs them
even though they are gone, to measure against.
The silver is worn down to the brass underneath
and is the better for it. He will gauge
by the smell of concrete sidewalks after night rain.
He is like an old ferry dragged on to the shore,
a home in its smashed grandeur, with the giant beams
and joists. Like a wooden ocean out of control.
A beached heart. A cauldron of cooling melt.

THE FRIENDSHIP INSIDE US

Why the mouth? Why is it the mouth we put to mouth
at the final moments? Why not the famous groin?
Because the groin is far away.
The mouth is close up against the spirit.
We couple desperately all night before setting out
for years in prison. But that is the body's goodbye.
We kiss the person we love last thing before
the coffin is shut, because it is our being
touching the unknown. A kiss is the frontier in us.
It is where the courting becomes the courtship,
where the dancing ends and the dance begins.
The mouth is our chief access to the intimacy
in which she may reside. Her mouth is the porch
of the brain. The forecourt of the heart.
The way to the mystery enthroned. Where we meet
momentarily amid the seraphim and the powers.

A THANKSGIVING DANCE

His spirit dances the long ago, and later.
Starlight on a country road in worn-out
western Pennsylvania. The smell of weeds
and rusting iron. And gladness.
His spirit welcomes the Italian New Year's
in a hill town filled with the music
of glass crashing everywhere in the cobbled
streets. Champagne and the first kisses.
Too shy to look at each other and no language
between them. He dances alone, the dance
of after that. Now they sit amid the heavy
Roman sunlight and talk of the people
they are married to now. He secretly
dances the waltz she was in her astonishing
beauty, drinking wine and laughing, the window
behind her filled with winter rain.

Our heart wanders lost in the dark woods.
Our dream wrestles in the castle of doubt.
But there's music in us. Hope is pushed down
but the angel flies up again taking us with her.
The summer mornings begin inch by inch
while we sleep, and walk with us later
as long-legged beauty through
the dirty streets. It is no surprise
that danger and suffering surround us.
What astonishes is the singing.
We know the horses are there in the dark
meadow because we can smell them,
can hear them breathing.
Our spirit persists like a man struggling
through the frozen valley
who suddenly smells flowers
and realizes the snow is melting
out of sight on top of the mountain,
knows that spring has begun.

IMMACULATE

The brain is dead and the body is
no longer infected by the spirit.
Now it is just machines talking
to the machine. Helping it back
to its old, pure journey.

MOREOVER

We are given the trees so we can know
what God looks like. And rivers
so we might understand Him. We are allowed
women so we can get into bed with the Lord,
however partial and momentary that is.
The passion, and then we are single again
while the dark goes on. He lived
in the Massachusetts woods for two years.
Went out naked among the summer pines
at midnight when the moon would allow it.
He watched the aspens when the afternoon breeze
was at them. And listened to rain
on the butternut tree near his window.
But when he finally left, they did not care.
The difficult garden he was midwife to
was indifferent. The eight wild birds
he fed through both winters, when the snow
was starving them, forgot him immediately.
And the three women he ate of and entered
utterly then and before, who were his New World
as immensity and landfall, are now only friends
or dead. What we are given is taken away,
but we manage to keep it secretly.
We lose everything, but make harvest
of the consequence it was to us. Memory
builds this kingdom from the fragments
and approximation. We are gleaners who fill
the barn for the winter that comes on.

A KIND OF DECORUM

It is burden enough that death lies on all sides,
that your old kimono is still locked in my closet.
Now I wonder what would happen if my life did
catch on fire again. Would I break in half,
part of me a storm and part like ice in a silver bowl?
I lie awake remembering the birds of Kyoto
calling *No No*, unh unh. *No No*, unh unh. And you
saying yes all night. You said yes when I woke you
again in the dawn. And even disgracefully
at lunchtime. Until all the men at the small inn
roamed about, hoping to see whoever that voice was.
The Buddha tells us we should clear every obstacle
out of the way. "If you meet your mother in the path,
kill her. If the Buddha gets in the way, kill him."
But my spirit sings like the perishing cicadas
while I sit in the back yard hitting an old pot.

A WALK BLOSSOMING

The spirit opens as life closes down.
Tries to frame the size of whatever God is.
Finds that dying makes us visible.
Realizes we must get to the loin of that
before time is over. The part of which
we are the wall around. Not the good or evil,
neither death nor afterlife but the importance
of what we contain meanwhile. (He walks along
remembering, biting into beauty,
the heart eating into the naked spirit.)
The body is a major nation, the mind is a gift.
Together they define substantiality.
The spirit can know the Lord as a flavor
rather than power. The soul is ambitious
for what is invisible. Hungers for a sacrament
that is both spirit and flesh. And neither.

FARMING IN SECRET

They piled the bound angels with the barley
in the threshing ring and drove the cow
and donkeys over them all day. Threw the mix
into the wind from the sea to separate
the blond meal from the gold of what
had been. It burned in the luminous air.
When the night came, the mound of grain
was almost higher than the farmhouse. But there
were only eight sacks of the other.

DECEMBER NINTH, 1960

Walked around Bologna at three in the morning.
Beautiful, arcaded, deserted piazza and winter rain.
Got the train at five of four. Slept badly
in a hot compartment, curled up on my half
of the seat. No real dawn. Beginning to see
a little into the mist. The looming mountain
brindled with snow. The higher pines crusted.
Oyster-white behind them. The train running along
a river between the hills. Mostly apple orchards
with occasionally pale apples still near the top.
Also vineyards. No feeling of Italy here.
No sense of the Umbrian peasants farming
with their white ocean. A tractor instead
putting out compost near an orchard with rotten
red squash gourds. Later another man standing
in the river with a long-handled net, looking
steadily down. Then the commuter line between
Bolzano and Merano. Changing pants on the toilet.
Checked my bag in the station and walked
to the center of the town. Hotels everywhere.
Mountain scenery in the summer, skiing in winter.
Went into the CIT and asked about Pound. (Because
the address had been left at home in Perugia.)
They said he was not there anymore. Went to
the tourist office. Herr Herschel said, yes, Pound
was still there. I came out chuckling, as though
I had been sly. Then, waiting for the first bus
to Tirolo. It leaves at ten-thirty. It's supposed
to be a half hour's walk from there.

NOT THE HAPPINESS BUT
THE CONSEQUENCE OF HAPPINESS

He wakes up in the silence of the winter woods,
the silence of birds not singing, knowing he will
not hear his voice all day. He remembers what
the brown owl sounded like while he was sleeping.
The man wakes in the frigid morning thinking
about women. Not with desire so much as with a sense
of what is not. The January silence is the sound
of his feet in the snow, a squirrel scolding,
or the scraping calls of a single blue jay.
Something of him dances there, apart and gravely mute.
Many days in the woods he wonders what it is
that he has for so long hunted down. We go hand
in hand, he thinks, into the dark pleasure,
but we are rewarded alone, just as we are married
into aloneness. He walks the paths doing the strange
mathematics of the brain, multiplying the spirit.
He thinks of caressing her feet as she kept dying.
For the last four hours, watching her gradually stop
as the hospital slept. Remembers the stunning
coldness of her head when he kissed her just after.
There is light or more light, darkness and less darkness.
It is, he decides, a quality without definition.
How strange to discover that one lives with the heart
as one lives with a wife. Even after many years,
nobody knows what she is like. The heart has
a life of its own. It gets free of us, escapes,
is ambitiously unfaithful. Dies out unaccountably
after eight years, blooms unnecessarily and too late.
Like the arbitrary silence in the white woods,
leaving tracks in the snow he cannot recognize.

INFIDELITY

She is never dead when he meets her.
They eat noodles for breakfast as usual.
For eleven years he thought it was the river
at the bottom of his mind dreaming.
Now he knows she is living inside him,
as the wind is sometimes visible
in the trees. As the roses and rhubarb
are in the garden and then not.
Her ashes are by the sea in Kamakura.
Her face and hair and sweet body still
in the old villa on a mountain where
she lived the whole summer. They slept
on the floor for eleven years.
But now she comes less and less.

THE REINVENTION OF HAPPINESS

I remember how I'd lie on my roof
listening to the fat violinist
below in the sleeping village
play Schubert so badly, so well.

LOOKING AT PITTSBURGH FROM PARIS

The boat of his heart is tethered to the ancient
stone bridges. Beached on the Pacific hills with
thick evening fog flooding whitely over the ridge.
Running in front of the Provençal summer. Drowned
as a secret under the broad Monongahela River.
Forever richly laden with Oak Street and Umbria.
"There be monsters," they warn in the blank spaces
of the old maps. But the real danger is the ocean's
insufficiency, the senseless repetition throughout
the empty waters. Calm and storms and calm again.
Too impoverished for the human. We come to know
ourselves as immense continents and archipelagoes
of endless bounty. He waits now in the hold
of a wooden ship. Becalmed, maybe standing to.
Bobbing, rocking softly. The cargo of ghosts
and angels all around. The wraiths, surprisingly,
singing with the clear voices of young boys.
The angels clapping the rhythm. As he watches
for morning, for the dark to give way and show
his landfall, the new country, his native land.

"MY EYES ADORED YOU"

She came into his life like arriving halfway
through a novel, with bits of two earlier lives
snagged in her. She was the daughter of
a deputy attorney general. And when
that crashed she tried singing and got married.
Now she is in trouble again, leaving soup
on his porch before really knowing him.
Saying she heard he had a bad cold, and besides
it was a tough winter. (It was like
his first wife who went to the department store
and bought a brass bed, getting a salesman
his size to lie down so she could see if it fit.
When she still knew him only at a distance.)
But when people grow up, they should know better.
You can't call it romance when she already had
two children. He had decided never again to get
involved with love. Now everything
has gone wrong. She doesn't just sing softly
up to his window. You can see them in the dark
upstairs, him singing badly and her not minding.

BEYOND PLEASURE

Gradually we realize what is felt is not so important
(however lovely or cruel) as what the feeling contains.
Not what happens to us in childhood, but what was
inside what happened. Ken Kesey sitting in the woods,
beyond his fence of whitewashed motorcycles, said when
he was writing on acid he was not writing about it.
He used what he wrote as blazes to find his way back
to what he knew then. Poetry registers
feelings, delights and passion, but the best searches
out what is beyond pleasure, is outside process.
Not the passion so much as what the fervor can be
an ingress to. Poetry fishes us to find a world
part by part, as the photograph interrupts the flux
to give us time to see each thing separate and enough.
The poem chooses part of our endless flowing forward
to know its merit with attention.

DUENDE

I can't remember her name.
It's not as though I've been in bed
with that many women.
The truth is I can't even remember
her face. I kind of know how strong
her thighs were, and her beauty.
But what I won't forget
is the way she tore open
the barbecued chicken with her hands,
and wiped the grease on her breasts.

THE GOOD LIFE

When he wakes up, a weak sun is just rising
over the side of the valley. It is eight
degrees below zero in the house.
He builds a fire and makes tea. Puts out seeds
for the birds and examines the tracks
in fresh snow, still trying to learn
what lives here. He is writing a poem
when his friend calls. She asks what
he plans to do today. To write some
letters, he tells her (because he is falling
behind in his project of writing one
every day for a month).
She tells him how many letters famous poets
write each day. Says she doesn't mean
that as criticism. After they hang up,
he stands looking at the unanswered mail
heaped high on the table. Gets back
in bed and starts reworking his poem.

FLAT HEDGEHOGS

FOR ISAIAH BERLIN

When the hedgehogs here at night
see a car and its fierce lights
coming at them, they do the one
big thing they know.

PROSPERO LISTENING TO THE NIGHT

The intricate vast process has produced
a singularity which lies in darkness
hearing the small owls, a donkey snorting
in the barley field, and frogs down near
the cove. What he is listening to is
the muteness of the dog at each farm
in the valley. Their silence means no
lover is abroad nor any vagrant looking
for where to sleep. But there is a young
man, very still, under the heavy grapes
in another part of Heaven. There are still
women hoping behind the dark windows
of farmhouses. Like he can hear himself not
hearing Verdi. What else don't the dogs know?

THE END OF PARADISE

When the angels found him sitting in the half light
of his kerosene lamp eating lentils, his eyes widened.
But all he said was could he leave a note. The one
wearing black looked at the one in red who shrugged,
so he began writing, desperately. Wadded the message
into an envelope and wrote *Anna* on the front. Quickly
began another, shoulders hunched, afraid of them.
Finished and wrote *Pimpaporn* on it. Began a third
one and the heavy angel growled. "I have Schubert,"
the man offered, turning on the tape. The one in black
said quietly that at least he didn't say "So soon!"
When the ink ran out, the man whimpered and struggled
to the table piled with books and drafts. He finished
again and scrawled *Suzanne* across it. The one in red
growled again and the man said he would put on his shoes.
When they took him out into the smell of dry vetch
and the ocean, he began to hold back, pleading:
"I didn't put the addresses! I don't want them to think
I forgot." "It doesn't matter," the better angel said,
"they have been dead for years."

THE LOST WORLD

Think what it was like, he said. Peggy Lee and Goodman
all the time. Carl Ravazza making me crazy
with "Vieni Su" from a ballroom in New Jersey
every night, the radio filling my dark room
in Pittsburgh with naked-shouldered women
in black gowns. Helen Forest and Helen O'Connell,
and later the young Sarah Vaughan out of Chicago
from midnight until two. Think of being fifteen
in the middle of leafy June when Sinatra and Ray
Eberle both had number-one records of "Fools Rush In."
Somebody singing "Tenderly" and somebody doing
"This Love of Mine." Helplessly adolescent while
the sound of romance was constantly everywhere.
All day long out of windows along the street.
Sinatra with "Close to You." And all the bands. Artie
Shaw with "Green Eyes" and whoever was always playing
"Begin the Beguine." Me desperate because I wouldn't
get there in time. Who can blame me for my heart?
What choice did I have? Harry James with "Sleepy
Lagoon." Imagine, on a summer night, "Sleepy Lagoon"!

MAYBE VERY HAPPY

After she died he was seized
by a great curiosity about what
it was like for her. Not that he
doubted how much she loved him.
But he knew there must have been
some things she had not liked.
So he went to her closest friend
and asked what she complained of.
"It's all right," he had to keep
saying, "I really won't mind."
Until the friend finally gave in.
"She said sometimes you made a noise
drinking your tea if it was very hot."

THE MANGER OF INCIDENTALS

We are surrounded by the absurd excess of the universe.
By meaningless bulk, vastness without size,
power without consequence. The stubborn iteration
that is present without being felt.
Nothing the spirit can marry. Merely phenomenon
and its physics. An endless, endless of going on.
No habitat where the brain can recognize itself.
No pertinence for the heart. Helpless duplication.
The horror of none of it being alive.
No red squirrels, no flowers, not even weed.
Nothing that knows what season it is.
The stars uninflected by awareness.
Miming without implication. We alone see the iris
in front of the cabin reach its perfection
and quickly perish. The lamb is born into happiness
and is eaten for Easter. We are blessed
with powerful love and it goes away. We can mourn.
We live the strangeness of being momentary,
and still we are exalted by being temporary.
The grand Italy of meanwhile. It is the fact of being brief,
being small and slight that is the source of our beauty.
We are a singularity that makes music out of noise
because we must hurry. We make a harvest of loneliness
and desiring in the blank wasteland of the cosmos.

THE THIRTY FAVORITE LIVES: AMAGER

I woke up every morning on the fourth floor,
in the two-hundred-year-old walls made
of plaster and river grass. I would leave
the woman and walk across beautiful København
to the island of Amager. To my small room
in the leftover Nazi barracks that looked out
on a swamp. Most of the time it was winter.
I would light my hydrant-size iron stove
and set a pot on top, putting in hamburger
and vegetables while the water was getting hot.
Starting to type with numb hands. The book
I planned to write in two weeks for a thousand
dollars already a week behind (and threatening
to get beyond a month). Out of money and no
prospects. Then the lovely smell of soup
and the room snug. I would type all day
and late into the night. Until the soup
was finished. Then I would start back across
the frozen city, crunching over the moats,
loud in the silence. The stars brilliant.
Focused on her waiting for me, ready to fry
sausages at two in the morning. Me thinking idly
of the ancient Chinese poet writing in his
poverty, "Ah, is this not happiness."

BURMA

Used, misled, cheated. Our time always shortening.
What we cherish always temporary. What we love
is, sooner or later, changed. But for a while we can
visit our other life. Can rejoice in its being there
in its absence. Giving thanks for what we are allowed
to think about it, grateful for it even as it wanes.
For knowing it is there. The way women on rainy days
sometimes go into the bedroom to cry about losing
the first man they loved. The way a man remembers the young
woman at an upstairs window looking out he saw once,
for a moment, as he drove through a sleeping village.
Or the brightness in the memory of the failed hotel
where the waiters in their immaculate white uniforms
were barefoot. The elegant dining room silent except for
the sound of rain falling in the tin buckets. And
the whispering of giant overhead fans with broken
blades as they turned in the heat. There was the scraping
sound in the piles of dead leaves on the lavish veranda.
And occasionally the bright sound of broken glass.
All of it a blessing. The being there. Being alive then.
Like a giant bell ringing long after you can't hear it.

WHAT I'VE GOT

After twenty hours in bed with no food, I decided
I should have at least tea. Got up to light the lamp,
but the sweating and shivering started again
and I staggered backwards across the room. Slammed
against the stone wall. Came to with blood on my head
and couldn't figure out which way the bed was.
Crawled around searching for the matches but gave up,
remembering there was one left in a box by the stove.
It flared and went out. "Exaggerated," I said
and groped back toward my desk, feeling for the matches
with barefoot geisha steps. Began to shake and moan,
my teeth chattering like the hero did in the old movie
when his malaria returned. I smiled but was worried.
No telephone and nobody going by out there in the field
I could call to. And God knows what I had. Realized
I was on all fours again. Interesting, something said
as I dragged myself onto the bed. Interesting?
another part said. Interesting! For Christ's sake!

TROUBLE

That is what the *Odyssey* means.
Love can leave you nowhere in New Mexico
raising peacocks for the rest of your life.
The seriously happy heart is a problem.
Not the easy excitement, but summer
in the Mediterranean mixed with
the rain and bitter cold of February
on the Riviera, everything on fire
in the violent winds. The pregnant heart
is driven to hopes that are the wrong
size for this world. Love is always
disturbing in the heavenly kingdom.
Eden cannot manage so much ambition.
The kids ran from all over the piazza
yelling and pointing and jeering
at the young Saint Chrysostom
standing dazed in the church doorway
with the shining around his mouth
where the Madonna had kissed him.

IN THE BEGINNING

In the morning when Eve and Adam
woke to snow and their minds,
they set out in marvelous clothes
hand in hand under the trees.

Endlessly precision met them,
until they went grinning in time
with no word for their close
escape from that warm monotony.

METIER

The Greek fishermen do not
play on the beach and I don't
write funny poems.

YLAPA

Having swum in the jungle pool
under the waterfall and struggled
down again through the wattle huts,
we still had three hours to wait
before the boat would go back.
The only foreigners had a gallery.
She was British and naked in her halter.
He also was standard, with his stubble
and drunken talk of sex at ten
in the morning. Telling us loudly
how she stayed with him because
of his three hundred a month. She waded
through their old hatred picking up
the sketches as each in turn blew down
in the wind running before the storm.

A TASTE FOR GRIT AND WHATEVER

More and more it is the incidental that makes
him yearn, and he worries about that.
Why should the single railroad tracks
curving away into the bare December trees
and no houses matter? And why is it
the defeated he trusts? Is it because
Pittsburgh is still tangled in him that he
has the picture on his wall of God's head
torn apart by jungle roots? Maybe
growing up in that brutal city left him
with a taste for grit and whatever it was
he saw in the titanic rusting steel mills.
It might be the reason he finally moved out
of Paris. Perhaps it is the scale
of those long ago winters that makes him
restless when people laugh a lot.
Why the erotic matters so much. Not as
pleasure but a way to get to something darker.
Hunting down the soul, searching out the iron
of Heaven when the work is getting done.

MAYBE SHE IS HERE

She might be here secretly.
On her hands and knees
with her head down a bit
tilted to peer around the doorjamb
in the morning, watching me
before I wake up.
Only her face showing
and her shoulders. In a slip,
her skin honey against the simple
white of two thin straps
and the worked edge of the bodice.
With her right hand a little visible.

The author wishes to thank Kerry O'Keefe and Henry Lyman for their assistance in preparing this book.

A NOTE ON THE TYPE

This book was set in Janson, a typeface long thought to have been made by the Dutchman Anton Janson, who was a practicing typefounder in Leipzig during the years 1668–1687. However, it has been conclusively demonstrated that these types are actually the work of Nicholas Kis (1650–1702), a Hungarian, who most probably learned his trade from the master Dutch typefounder Dirk Voskens. The type is an excellent example of the influential and sturdy Dutch types that prevailed in England up to the time William Caslon (1692–1766) developed his own incomparable designs from them.

COMPOSED BY CREATIVE GRAPHICS,

ALLENTOWN, PENNSYLVANIA

PRINTED AND BOUND BY UNITED BOOK PRESS,

BALTIMORE, MARYLAND

DESIGNED BY ROBERT C. OLSSON